JAMES BALDWIN
(1924–1987)

The Life and Times of James Baldwin

Derek Kali

TABLE OF CONTENT

INTRODUCTION

James Baldwin became a prominent voice, particularly in the late 1950s and early 1960s, in the United States and, later, across most of western Europe, through his eloquence and passion for the subject of race in America.

His parents had nine children, of whom he was the eldest. His childhood was marked by poverty in the Black Harlem neighborhood of New York City. It was during his teens that he first experienced evangelism when he took on the role of a preacher in a small revivalist church.

He described this era in his autobiographical novel Go Tell It on the Mountain (1953) and in his one-act play The Amen Corner (1957). (performed in New York City, 1965).

During his post-high school years, he had a period of intermittent and poorly compensated jobs, self-study, and short-term literary apprenticeships in Greenwich Village, the well-known bohemian area of New York City.

He went to Paris for the next eight years after he left in 1948. Later in his life, he described himself as a "transatlantic commuter," and from that point on, lived in France and the US. Giovanni's Room is a book about the white world.

The story centers on an American living in Paris who grapples with a deep inner conflict about whether to choose love for a man or love for a woman. A compilation of short stories, Sketches of a Native Son, resulted from the publication of the two novels (1955).

From the mid-1950s onward, he returned to the United States and joined the nation's civil rights movement. In Nobody Knows My Name: Black-White Relations in the United States (1961), the author attempts to analyze racial tensions in the United States. Sexual as well as racial themes are addressed in his 1962 novel, Another Country, which is also related to this theme.

Almost all of the November 17, 1962, issue of The New Yorker was dedicated to a lengthy essay by writer James Baldwin, who focused on Black Muslim separatist groups and other civil rights activities. The essay skyrocketed to the top of the New York Times Best Seller list as The Fire Next Time (1963).

In 1964, his angry blues against racism, "Blues for Mister Charlie," received mixed reviews while it was running on Broadway.

Though Baldwin wrote until his death, none of his later works achieved the same level of success as his earlier work.

JAMES BALDWIN

James Baldwin was an essayist, dramatist, novelist, and civil rights movement activist whose most well-known work is' Notes of a Native Son. '

Go Tell It on the Mountain was Baldwin's major work, and he used it to bring race, spirituality, and humanity to the forefront of public discourse. Other books, like Giovanni's Room, Just Above My Head, and Another Country, were also included, while articles like Notes of a Native Son and The Fire Next Time were included as well.

Pre-adolescence

James Baldwin, who was born on August 2, 1924, in Harlem, New York, was a writer and playwright. In addition to breaking new ground, one of the finest 20th-century writers,

Baldwin wrote about racial and social themes in a number of his works. For a while, he was especially known for his articles on the African-American experience in the United States.

When Baldwin was born, his mother was a young single woman and gave birth to him in Harlem Hospital. It is believed that she never revealed the name of his biological father to him.

When James was three years old, he was married to David Baldwin, a Baptist clergyman.

Even when their relationship was poor, Baldwin followed in his stepfather's footsteps.

This was due to the fact that he always referred to him as his father, despite the fact that he had not given him a son.

From the ages of 14 to 16, he served as a youth minister in a Harlem Pentecostal church.

Baldwin was drawn to literature at a young age, and his writing showed promise when he was in school. He graduated from DeWitt Clinton High School in the Bronx, where he and future famed photographer Richard Avedon worked on the school's magazine.

Baldwin started out as a very young writer who was eager to use literary tropes not normally seen in young writers.

In order to support his family of seven younger children, he had to put his aspirations for college on hold. He was determined to locate work as, no matter where he found it, he would lay railroad tracks for the U.S. Army in New Jersey.

Even though he suffered discrimination because he was African American, Baldwin was often refused entry to restaurants, pubs, and other venues because of his race. Baldwin searched for other work following his firing from the New Jersey job, and struggled to make ends meet.

BALDWIN WRITES

Baldwin lost his father on July 29, 1943, and received an eighth sibling at the same time. He immediately relocated to Greenwich Village, an artists' haven in the City.

In order to devote himself to writing a novel, Baldwin took a series of odd jobs in order to earn a living. He met and befriended Richard Wright, who provided him with a scholarship so he could pursue graduate studies in 1945. Shortly after publishing his first short stories and articles in magazines such as The Nation, Partisan Review, and Commentary, Baldwin found his writing appearing in other national publications, such as The Nation, Partisan Review, and Commentary.

While Baldwin remained in the city three years later, he dramatically changed his life and relocated to Paris on a fellowship. Baldwin moved to a different neighborhood, allowing him to write about his personal and racial history in greater detail.

"I understand how far I've come now that I've crossed the ocean...

My lineage traces to those who were once enslaved, and I am a writer. Both have to be dealt with. " A recent interview with The New York Times quotes Baldwin as saying. He entered the "transatlantic commuter" phase of his life when he started living on both sides of the Atlantic.

Go Tell It on the Mountain was Baldwin's first book to be published. The autobiographical story featured a young man from Harlem navigating his relationship with his father and religion as he grew up.

"I have only ever written one book, and it is about mountains. I had to focus on the thing that caused me the most pain. For a long time, I had to cope with my father above everything, "In later comments, he stated.

Gay fiction

The Guggenheim Fellowship was awarded to Baldwin in 1954. The next year, he published his new work, titled Giovanni's Room. The piece showcased a complicated picture of homosexuality and broke new ground for a subject that was considered taboo at the time.

Baldwin's later novel, Just Above My Head, similarly deals with the subject of love between men (1978). Another Country also tackled interracial relationships, which were somewhat contentious at the time, as the story makes apparent.

He didn't care who he slept with as long as the relationship was mutually pleasurable. Nonetheless, he was firm in his belief that categorizing human sexuality was the cause of restricting freedom, and that sexual identity is more fluid and less rigid than expressed in the United States.

In a 1969 interview, the writer claimed that "being gay is an anomaly" and that such ideas show that people are narrow-minded and stagnant.

People know me as 'Nobody Knows My Name'.

Baldwin became widely known for his writing for the stage after authoring numerous plays. The Amen Corner, which took a close look at the phenomenon of storefront Pentecostal ism, was written by him. Howard University staged the play in 1955, and it was later revived on Broadway in the mid-1960s.

But it was his articles, and in particular his pieces on racism, that established Baldwin as one of the era's greatest authors. (1961).

Nobody Knows My Name sold over a million copies, and became a bestseller. While not an activist that marches or sits, Baldwin's role in the Civil Rights Movement was extraordinary because of his powerful writing on race.

BALDWIN IN FRANCE

In hopes of finishing his first novel, Go Tell It On The Mountain, which he began writing in 1948 in Paris, France, Baldwin traveled to Paris in 1948 in order to finish the work and complete his Notes of a Native Son (1955).

The young author landed in Paris with only forty dollars in his pocket at the age of twenty-four. While in the United States, he fell in love with the city due to its beauty and culture, as well as due to the respite it provided from the discriminatory racial and sexual conditions he experienced in the country. Baldwin's mind was set free as a result of this design.

His primary work was done here in Mississippi and in Switzerland, where he finished writing Go Tell It On The Mountain. While in Paris, Baldwin had various sources of inspiration for his fictitious characters. As a backdrop for his second work, the city supplies Giovanni's Room (1956).

Baldwin resided in several modest hotels in the Saint-Germain region of Paris, which was an artists' and writers' neighborhood from the 1940s to the 1950s. Here, Baldwin discovered a community of talented people of many backgrounds.

The social scene in that neighborhood provided him with a little reprieve from the stressful everyday routine that came with living in the United States. Jean-Paul Sartre, Albert Camus, and Simone de Beauvoir are among the many French intellectuals who worked and socialized at the Café de Flore, where writing and socializing went hand-in-hand.

The pubs and nightclubs provided a setting where the effusive Baldwin could dance, sing, laugh, and discover his sexuality, where he could do it with other people supportive of him.

In Paris, where he spent long and short stays, Baldwin became Baldwin's first international home. However, the city of Paris was also a major cause of turmoil. Once, after Baldwin had moved to France, he had a falling out with his mentor and friend, the writer Richard Wright.

When Baldwin wrote an essay for the French magazine, Zero, in 1949, Wright felt personally offended. Baldwin suggests in his essay, "Everybody's Protest Novel," that the protest novel genre fails the reader by failing to represent the real world as accurately as possible.

He offers Wright's Native Son (1940) as an example and contrasts it with Uncle Tom's Cabin (1852), a very controversial slave narrative that became known as Uncle Tom's Cabin. This incensed Wright, who believed that Baldwin was picking on him personally.

Their friendship was never entirely healed as a result of their public argument in Paris. While regretting their departure, Baldwin did not reconsider his thoughts on Bigger Thomas, the protagonist of Native Son.

His final residence in St. Paul de Vence was granted to him by the South of France when he recovered from his illness and melancholy brought on by the assassinations of Medgar Evers, Malcolm X, and Martin Luther King, Jr.

The entrance of James Baldwin in 1971 to the little village in Provence was not met with enthusiasm. Baldwin biographer Jules B. Farber, according to a friend of Baldwin's, remembered that when Baldwin first arrived at St. Paul-de-Vence, all the white Presbyterians from the city of St. Paul-de-Vence looked at him with suspicion since he was black and gay. However, soon after he began living among the peasants, his outgoing attitude began to draw them to him.

After listening to him, one of the interviewees, Betrand Mazodier, remembered the level of respect that emerged soon after:

The locals are mostly simple people who chat about farmwork, orchard/vineyard farming, fruit-tree growing, the weather, and their favourite beverage. Baldwin, with his open-mindedness, his keen wit, and his beguiling grin, rapidly became a fixture in Saint-Paul's life. Most of the people who live here are quite well-known, yet they tend to keep to themselves, preferring not to interact with the locals. He was the one notable exception. He made an extra effort to engage and speak with anybody he met in town.

He additionally became more well-known after meeting and befriending Simone Signoret, a well-known French actress. After he was recuperated, she invited him to stay in St. Paul and got him a place to reside with a woman named Mlle. Jeanne Faure, who didn't want to house a black guy. She acquired a strong fondness for Baldwin over time, but eventually, she began to respect him as well. As he spent a significant amount of money renting numerous rooms in the house, he finally became the owner of the huge eighteenth-century home, purchasing it with money he received from his books.

People were essential to Baldwin's life, and he had a never-ending desire to keep other people around him. As a result, he was going to soon become a well-received guest at the La Colombe d'Or, a neighboring inn owned by the Roux family. His acquaintances and friends from the community were invited to join him for meals and beverages at the inn, as well as those he met on his daily walks. While serving as the head of Baldwin's healthcare for nearly 10 years, Dr. Roger Boizard became a trusted companion to Baldwin, who enjoyed meals and beverages with him several times a week.

When Baldwin lived in St. Paul de Vence, he grew close to the village residents who had migrated there. The French-American sculptor Armand Arman, who was born in St. Thomas in the Virgin Islands, and his wife Corice Canton, were among the friends who accompanied Brer

Rabbit. This group also included Wanda and Dick van Dijk, from the Netherlands, and fellow author Nicholas Delbanco, who was born in London.

THE FIRE NEXT TIME

Baldwin saw a major transformation in his artistic approach when the novel The Fire Next Time was released in 1963. This book of essays was created to teach white Americans about the subject of being black. In addition, it gave African Americans the opportunity to see themselves through the eyes of white readers.

The depictions of race relations in Baldwin's book were strikingly true, but he nevertheless expressed hope for a better future. And if we fail in our duty today, we might yet be able to put an end to the race war. He's capable of having an impact on the American people; as a result, The Fire Next Time was among the best-selling books of all time.

Baldwin appeared on the cover of Time magazine in the same year. A quote from the Time magazine article: "There is no other writer — white or black — who is able to grasp so acutely and bluntly the deeper complexities of the racial conflagration that is occurring in the North and South," the article says.

As a direct result of his successful previous play, Blues for Mister Charlie, Baldwin wrote another, and this one premiered on Broadway in 1964. The plot is partially based on the 1955 racially motivated murder of Emmett Till, a 14-year-old African American kid from Chicago who was murdered while visiting family in Mississippi.

The same year, his book with Avedon, which had been a project for some time, was finally released to the public. The piece was dedicated to the assassinated civil rights activist Medgar Evers. Other publications include collections of short stories, such as Going to Meet the Man, that Baldwin published around this time.

To broaden the scope of his book, in his 1968 novel Tell Me How Long the Train's Been Gone, Baldwin explored issues such as sexuality, family, and the African-American experience. Some commentators criticized the book, saying it was an ideologically charged diatribe rather than a work of fiction. Even though many critics disliked his narration of the book as "I," he also faced criticism for his tendency to use the first-person singular, "I."

The mid-1970s seemed to bring Baldwin to the brink of despair with regard to race relations. For most of the preceding decade, he had witnessed an abundance of violence as a result of racial hatred, including the assassinations of Medgar Evers, Malcolm X, and Martin Luther King Jr.

His paintings exhibit a harsher tone, especially compared to earlier ones. The controversy surrounding No Name in the Street, a 1972 book of essays, has often been cited as the beginning of the transformation in Baldwin's writing. He also worked on a screenplay based on the book "The Autobiography of Malcolm X" at this time, hoping to turn it into a film.

Baldwin produced new works in a variety of forms as his literary popularity waned slightly during his latter years. Jimmy's Blues: Selected Poems was published in 1983 and the 1987 novel Harlem Quartet as well.

Additionally, Baldwin continued to examine race and American culture with keen perceptiveness. From the evidence found in the Atlanta child murders, he produced The Evidence of Things Not Seen in 1985. He spent many years as a college professor talking about his experiences and perspectives. He taught at the University of Massachusetts at Amherst and Hampshire College for years before his death.

On December 1, 1987, Baldwin passed away at his residence in St. Paul de Vence, France. Baldwin's primary aim was to bear testimony to the truth; he never wanted to be a speaker or a leader. Through his expansive and devoted literary legacy, he managed to accomplish this aim.

www.ingramcontent.com/pod-product-compliance
Ingram Content Group UK Ltd.
Pitfield, Milton Keynes, MK11 3LW, UK
UKHW022008190726
13853UKWH00004B/1801

9 798548 639493